The Little Book of

NEWCASTLE
UNITED

CARLTON
BOOKS

This edition published in 2007
First published by Carlton Books in 2003

A CIP catalogue record for this book is available
from the British Library.

ISBN 978 1 84442 859 5

Printed in Singapore

INTRODUCTION

There is no other club like this.
For a century Newcastle have found
new ways to amaze, frustrate, delight
and exasperate their supporters.
This book attempts the impossible task
of conveying that history via a collection
of quotes, both from the greats and
from those best forgotten.
But in the end there's only really one,
universally acknowledged, quote about
this club that needs to be recorded:

'Howay the Lads'

❝It was agreed that the club's colours should be changed from red shirts and white knickers to black-and-white shirts (two-inch stripe) and dark knickers.**❞**

Minutes of club meeting, 2.8.1894

❝I have been sold like a slave
for a bag of gold.**❞**

Hughie Gallacher *reacts badly to being
transferred to Chelsea, 1930*

❛Hughie of the Magic Feet is Dead❜

*Headline in the **Newcastle Journal**, 12.6.57, following the suicide of Hughie Gallacher*

"Good evening, Newcastle!"

David Bowie *greets the crowd from the stage of…*
Roker Park, Glass Spider Tour, 23.6.87

❝I may have looked calm but my backside was going some.**❞**

Alan Shearer *after his successful penalty in the FA Cup semi-final v Spurs, 11.3.99*

❝Let's kill off once and for all the rumours that Ossie's job is on the line…**❞**

Sir John Hall *allays fears that Ardiles will be sacked, 2.4.92*

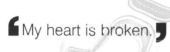

'My heart is broken.**'**

Ossie Ardiles *reacts to his sacking as manager,*
5.4.92

If you put 11 black-and-white dogs on the field at Newcastle you'd get 30,000 coming to watch.

Sir Matt Busby

❝I picked up an injury and spent quite a lot of time on the bench. One of the supporters knitted me a cushion to sit on, which said, 'Reserved for Brian Kilcline'.**❞**

The man also known as **'Killer'** *on home comforts at St James' Park*

❝It will always rankle with me that we didn't take the title after being so close, but I maintain that Manchester United won it rather than us losing it. **❞**

Rob Lee *on the lasting disappointment of season 1995–96, when the wrong United won the title*

'Happy Birthday – any chance of a rise?'

*Message from **Alan Shearer** in a card marking Sir Bobby Robson's 70th birthday*

❝Robson the man I don't really know. I just know Robson the manager.**❞**

Newcastle chairman, **Freddy Shepherd**, *explains his relationship with Bobby Robson*

❮ He saved my career in a way, because I was down in the dumps when he came to Newcastle – he got me back to playing the way that I know I can. **❯**

Alan Shearer *on Bobby Robson*

❛I wish we had supporters like Newcastle's. Their supporters are more loyal than ours. One has to be fair – if we'd signed Kevin Keegan, I don't believe we would have had the same reaction through the turnstiles. ❜

*Sunderland chairman **Tom Cowie** and his envy of Tyneside, 1982*

❝Our prices are half Newcastle's prices – you just can't compare the clubs, they're not to compare. We're stuck between a massive city that's vibrant like Newcastle… and Middlesbrough.**❞**

Sunderland chairman **Bobby Murray** *and his envy of Tyneside, 2002*

❛I prefer it in Newcastle, knowing all the people want me here. They look me in the eye and say, 'I want to play with you.'**❜**

David Ginola *loses something in the translation*

❛The added benefits of the new kit will give Newcastle an edge on the field of play and the white socks will give us an advantage over the opposition.**❜**

Ruud Gullit's *fashion forecasts prove to be a tad optimistic as United flop under his leadership*

❝ Mr Keegan, I've never seen such quality football played at such a pace in my life. **❞**

*Royal Antwerp coach, **Urbain Haesaert**, after NUFC's 5–0 win in Belgium, 13.9.94*

❛It's like a drug to them, they can't get enough of it. You've got to remember these fans have driven down motorways and watched some really abysmal sides in Newcastle shirts.❜

Kevin Keegan *tries to explain 'Toon Army mania'*

❝The last exciting piece of the jigsaw...❞

Kevin Keegan *upon signing Andy Cole*

❝We came out of the blocks like a Powderhall sprinter.**❞**

Kevin Keegan *reflects on the run of 11 league wins at the start of 1992–93*

'McEwans Best Scotch!'

John Hendrie, *when asked what made him come to Newcastle in 1988*

❝This is the only club I'd come back to just to sweep the terraces.**❞**

Jim Iley, *Magpies stalwart of the 1960s*

❛I'd give all this up tonight if it meant that Newcastle, come twenty to five on Saturday, were still in the Second Division.**❜**

John Anderson *after his testimonial match, April 1992, with the club deep in relegation trouble*

❝ There were four of us. We'd go and watch Newcastle play and, in the evening, we'd go to the all-in wrestling at St James' Hall. **❞**

Lifelong Toon fan **Cardinal Basil Hume**

❝If I've got it wrong then there's a bullet with my name on it.**❞**

Kevin Keegan *faces fans the day after selling top-scorer Andy Cole*

❝ None of you have any reason to doubt Kevin Keegan or me. We've taken the club from nothingness; we're on course to becoming one of the top three in the UK, the top 10 in Europe. **❞**

Sir John Hall, *the following day at the training ground*

❛ To call football religion is too much. But there's no doubt that, in places like Newcastle, when they've got a good team and are playing well, then the spirits of the people are lifted. **❜**

Cardinal Basil Hume *on football's place in the scheme of things*

❛People remember the occasion with great affection but not really the team.**❜**

*Journalist **John Gibson** on the men who beat Ujpest Dozsa in the Fairs Cup Final, 1969*

❝He was never a tactical genius but he did a marvellous job of managing Newcastle United.**❞**

Frank Clark *on Joe Harvey*

❝All you've got to do is score a goal. These foreigners are all the same, they'll collapse like a pack of cards – they've no gumption. **❞**

Joe Harvey's *inspirational half-time team talk in the Fairs Cup final second leg, 1969*

❝If Newcastle win promotion, forget about making Kevin Keegan Player of the Year – he'll deserve to be named Team of the Year. They should rename Newcastle, Keegan United.❞

Bob Paisley, *Liverpool boss, November 1983*

❝I wanted to wear that number nine shirt and nothing was going to derail me from getting it.**❞**

Alan Shearer

❛My eventual dream is to have 11 Geordies playing for Newcastle United and 11 in the reserves. ❜

Sir John Hall

❝ Toon army, Malcolm Macdonald, Kevin Keegan, John Hall and Julie's Nightclub! **❞**

*Sky TV pundit **Andy Gray**, when asked to name the five things that come to mind on hearing the word Newcastle*

❝You can't force people to sit down even if they have a seat. They want to sing and, unless you're Val Doonican, you can't do that sitting down.❞

Kevin Keegan, *1992*

'We're like the Basques. We are fighting for a nation, the Geordie nation. Football is tribalism and we're the Mohicans.'

Sir John Hall, *1995*

❝Of all 22 I was the only player born within the City walls and north of the Tyne. These lads from Durham and Chester-le-Street don't count.**❞**

Boyhood Toon fan **Denis Tueart** *after scoring the winner for Manchester City in the 1976 League Cup Final*

❝It's been everything I hoped for and more playing for Newcastle. The only – and it's a big only – thing that's missing is the silverware. Everything else has been fantastic.❞

Alan Shearer

❝ The pinnacle of my career has to be wearing the number nine for Newcastle, probably the most famous shirt in British football. I still have one stored under my bed. ❞

Tony Cunningham, *crowd favourite of the 1980s*

❝ Newcastle United have the worst PR of any major club in the country. **❞**

Fans champion **Rogan Taylor** *upon his appointment at Newcastle to try and improve relations with supporters*

❝He didn't actually cut his head off.**❞**

Fergie *responds to Roy Keane's dismissal after a clash with Alan Shearer, 15.9.01*

"He's grinning. "You prick".
He gestures dismissively.
The red card comes out.
Shearer's right.
I am a prick."

Roy Keane's *version of the same incident in*
his autobiography

❝But when we went up, it dawned on me what that really meant. I would have to go to Newcastle the following season as a Sunderland player. I couldn't do that.**❞**

Toon diehard **Lee Clark,** *later spotted at the 1998 FA Cup Final in a 'Sad Mackem Bastards' T-shirt*

❝Sad and miserable,
but very effective.**❞**

Bobby Robson *on Wimbledon after they'd beaten
Newcastle 2–0*

❛We've got to batten down the hatches, plug a few leaks and get the ship sailing again.**❜**

Robson *takes over HMS Newcastle United*

❝I have known Bobby Robson for a long time, but Newcastle are not the sort of club I am looking for. **❞**

Boudewijn Zenden – *within two years he had joined Middlesbrough*

"We promised we would help Newcastle United and we did."

Roberto Bettega, *Juventus vice-president, after Juve's victory in Kiev, which helps put United into the second round of the Champions League, 2002*

❛ I'm pretty ecstatic – but I'm pretty numb as well, so I'm a bit of both. **❜**

Bobby Robson *after victory at Feyenoord gives Newcastle a chance of qualification for the Champions League second round, 2002*

❮When I came, people asked me if I knew how big the job was. Now I know what they meant.**❯**

Gullit *resigns, 28.8.99*

❝I'm looking for a goalkeeper
with three legs.**❞**

Bobby Robson *after Shay Given is nutmegged
twice by Marcus Bent of Ipswich Town*

❛I can't sit there laughing, can I? Is that what you want? Ha ha ha – like that? Oh, penalty, ha ha. Oh, it's saved. Ha ha. No, it's gone in. Ha ha. What do you expect me to look like?**❜**

Bobby Robson's *reply to a journalist querying his downcast expression, 2003*

❝We're in a dog fight, and the fight in the dog will get us out of trouble. We are solid behind each other, and through being solid we will get out of trouble and, if that fails, then we will be in trouble, but that's not the situation here. We'll all get in the same rowing boat, and we'll all pick up an oar and we'll row the boat.❞

Bobby Robson *in Churchillian mode, 2003*

> **❝** The people here love their football and, if you play for Newcastle, they see you as a very special person. **❞**

Nolberto Solano

‘For Newcastle United, the sooner they knock down this place the better.**’**

Alan Shearer *on the demolition of Wembley*

❝And they were lucky
to get none.**❞**

Len Shackleton *after the 13–0 defeat of Newport
County, 5.10.46*

❝ Congratulations, I've heard a lot about you. But whatever you do, don't get injured. **❞**

New United boss **Bobby Robson** *meets Kieron Dyer – on the pitch at Wembley before England v Luxembourg, 1999*

❝ If you asked what would be my one wish, it would be to go back to England and, in one mad, great year, take over one club and win the championship. And I'd feel, well, I'd done it. **❞**

Then manager of Porto, **Bobby Robson** *hints at a return to the old country*

We mustn't be despondent. We don't have to play them every week – although we do play them next week as it happens.

Bobby Robson *after a 2–0 league defeat to Arsenal who United face a week later in the FA Cup*

‘ Bellamy came on at Liverpool and did well, but everyone thinks that he's the saviour, that he's Jesus Christ. He's not Jesus Christ. ’

Bobby Robson *debunks an unlikely myth*

❝They can't be monks – we don't want them to be monks; we want them to be football players because a monk doesn't play football at this level.**❞**

Bobby Robson *on the habits of his playing staff*

❝If we invite any player up to the quayside to see the girls and then up to our magnificent stadium, we will be able to persuade any player to sign.❞

Bobby Robson *on the myriad attractions of Tyneside*

❝ Of all the clubs I played for, I still get tingles down the back of my neck thinking about Newcastle. **❞**

Mickey Quinn, *former striker*

'At Newcastle I was older than the manager, older than the assistant manager, older than the physio and the club doctor – which must be some sort of record. '

Stuart Pearce *recounts life as captain of Newcastle's Dad's Army*

❝When I arrived, the fans called me a thieving Spaniard and a bloody gypsy who was robbing the club's cash.**❞**

Marcelino, *who is unlikely to return to the North-East on holiday*

‹ I haven't had any complaints from my neighbours yet but maybe that's because they're all Newcastle supporters – I'm just waiting to see what happens if we get any mackems moving into the neighbourhood. **›**

Lomana LuaLua *on his fondness for playing loud music*

❮I took him off because he wasn't hungry enough for his hat-trick.**❯**

*Hardman **Arthur Cox** explains why he substituted two-goal Chris Waddle, 1983*

❝I'm just a sheet metal worker's
son from Gosforth.**❞**

Alan Shearer, *local hero, 1996*

The circus came to town but the lions and tigers didn't turn up.

Kevin Keegan *after losing at Old Trafford in December 1995*

❝ He's not a player you can tell
to do this or do that, you just
have to let him get on with it. **❞**

Kevin Keegan *after Tino Asprilla's debut,*
February 1996

❝I've been out of short trousers for a long time now and I'm not going to say this is the worst day of my life.**❞**

Kenny Dalglish *after being sacked, August 1998*

'We're developing our youth
policy.**'**

Kenny Dalglish *after Ian Rush joined fellow
veteran John Barnes in Toon*

❝I know the players I want. It is like I have them in the fridge waiting to come out.**❞**

Ruud Gullit *gives his current squad the cold shoulder*

When he first came he wanted to get a fishing boat so they took him to Tynemouth the first weekend he was here. He took one look at the North Sea and said, 'F**k that!'

Tino Asprilla's interpreter **Nick Emerson**

❛ *Vaya cuidad – what a town!* **❜**

Tino Asprilla *after his first visit to Newcastle's famous Bigg Market*

❝ If we as a club – or Bill McGarry as an individual – had wanted a black-and-white army we would have introduced conscription. **❞**

Club programme editorial after crowd trouble at Hillsborough, 1980

Three goals – not bad.

Tino Asprilla's *appraisal of his stunning hat-trick against Barcelona, 1997*

❝ I was very happy, not angry, when I scored and I always celebrate in an unusual way. I threw it to a good fan and I would have got another from the bench. I knew what I was doing. Everyone congratulated me in the dressing room. ❞

Temuri Ketsbaia *on his manic hoarding-abusing goal celebration versus Bolton, 1998*

❝I haven't resigned; my mother hasn't got chicken pox; I haven't bought a house; I haven't been offered a job with the national team; I haven't been offered a job in America; I'm still here; my wife is okay; my daughter is okay; the groundsman is okay; everybody at Newcastle is okay.❞

Ruud Gullit, *21.8.99, a week before his resignation*

❝ Newcastle had not won in 29 games and two plus nine is 11. While they were scoring the winning goals, I was running round the outside of the ground 11 times to lift the hoodoo. I arrived late and had no ticket. But the moment I got out of the car and touched the Highbury stadium, Ray Parlour was sent off. ❞

Uri Geller *takes all the credit for ending Newcastle's thirty-game winless run in London, December 2001*

❝ That's the way I am and I always will be. After all, I kick Laurent Robert in training – and he's one of our players. **❞**

Andrew Griffin *on his no-nonsense philosophy*

❝ It was f****n' magic! When big Dunc Ferguson scored, I bloody exploded oot me seat, and so did Keegan! **❞**

AC/DC Singer **Bryan Johnson** *recalls a visit to see his beloved black and whites*

❝ The commission accepted that the incident was initially caused by Neil Lennon pulling at the shirt of Alan Shearer turning round and trapping his leg. It further accepted that the alleged incident of Alan Shearer swinging out with his left leg was a genuine attempt to free himself. ❞

Alan Shearer is cleared of assaulting Leicester City's Neil Lennon, 2000

This is a fantastic football club with great spirit and a public that live, breathe and die for everything that goes on here.

A defiant **Bobby Robson** *after United's loss to Partizan Belgrade, 2003*

❝I don't care if they ban me or fine me. Fine me what you like – I will pay it and I will still be right. I know I am right. Never in all my career have I seen a referee influence a game like that. He destroyed it, and I blame him for us losing the game. I can't blame it on myself, my team or Aston Villa. It was the referee and nothing else.**❞**

*An incandescent **Ruud Gullit** reacts to Alan Shearer's red card, 1999*

❛We want to make it a real East End night, with bangers and mash and lager and a lot of noise.**❜**

Leyton Orient chairman **Barry Hearn** *before the League Cup clash at Brisbane Road, 2000. United won 3–1 on aggregate*

❝I hated it. The f***ing fans were a bag of shit, the players weren't worth a light. I used to be at the dogs all the time. I bought a couple of greyhounds and thought, "F**k football".❞

*Striker **Billy Whitehurst** on his mixed memories of Newcastle*

'We tried everything to get him. Maybe they offered Sharon Stone.**'**

Tottenham manager **Ossie Ardiles** *on failing to get Philippe Albert, signed by Kevin Keegan*

❝ I've only got two words for how we played out there tonight – not good enough. **❞**

Bobby Robson

❝You never sell the fur of a bear before you shoot it. I have brought my cannon with me.❞

*A cryptic **Ruud Gullit** on his bid to sign Ibrahim Ba*

" The Geordie nation – that's what we're fighting for! London's the enemy! You exploit us, you use us. **"**

Sir John Hall

❝I don't f**king believe it!❞

Malcolm Allison's *live commentary on Century Radio, as Les Ferdinand scores Newcastle's winner against Middlesbrough, 1996*

❜ I've kept really quiet, but I'll tell you something, he went down in my estimation when he said that. But I'll tell ya – you can tell him now if you're watching it – we're still fighting for this title, and he's got to go to Middlesbrough and get something, and… and I tell you honestly, I will love it if we beat them… love it! ❜

Kevin Keegan *feels the heat coming from Alex Ferguson's direction during the Premiership run-in, 1996*

❝ This club should be buying players like Gascoigne and Beardsley, not selling them. If you sell class players like that you cannot keep producing them from out the bushes. **❞**

Kevin Keegan

❛… Tudor got it away to Hibbitt… Macdonald is on ahead… what a ball there by Hibbitt and away goes Macdonald again… and that's a magnificent goal! That is number two and that is the killer goal! **❜**

*The late **Brian Moore** describes Newcastle's second goal against Burnley in the 1974 FA Cup semi-final*

‟As the manager I have a duty to give them sweat, to give them blood and, to be quite honest, I would die for the club that I worked for. „

Gordon Lee *pledges his life to United, literally*

❝If I've done it wrong, I'm sorry but I think I did it right and time will show that I did it right.❞

*An unrepentant **Jack Charlton** interviewed after his resignation as manager*

'Not a team sheet but a suicide note.'

*Journalist **Tim Rich's** comment after Ruud Gullit omits Alan Shearer from his team to face Sunderland, 1999*

❛There was no hiding the fact that me and Ruud didn't see eye to eye, but I was as surprised as anyone when I heard the news. I always said no individual is bigger than any football club.**❜**

Alan Shearer's *reaction to Gullit's departure three days after losing the Tyne-Wear derby*

“Radford – now Tudor's gone down for Newcastle… Radford again, oh what a goal, what a goal!”

John Motson *launches his career as a football commentator by describing Hereford's equaliser in the FA Cup, February 1972*

‘ Nobody hands you cups on a plate. ,

Terry McDermott, *number two to Kevin Keegan*

❝How did we get on?❞

*Midfielder **Kevin Brock's** question to team-mates on the way back from Birmingham in 1992. He'd ended up in goal and taken a kick in the head for his troubles. United won 3–2*

'The only Irishman who didn't know where Dublin was.'

Unnamed reporter on Radio 5 Live after Shay Given failed to spot Coventry's No.9 lurking when he put the ball down in his own area. Dublin scored

❝ Surely Bobby Robson could have phoned me. After being involved in the international set-up for ten years, surely I'm worth a ten pence phone call. **❞**

Kevin Keegan *on the abrupt curtailment of his England career*

❝ The chant from the crowd, if you can follow the Geordie accents, appears to be, "Bobby Robson, are you watching on the box?" ❞

Tony Gubba *as Keegan scored four at Rotherham after being dropped by England manager Robson*

❛May 4, 1974, will haunt me for ever. I feel sick and embarrassed. **❜**

Joe Harvey *speaking about the 1974 FA Cup Final humiliation versus Liverpool*

❝I remember crouching down and crying at the end of the game and Bill Shankly came across and he put his arm around me and said, "Dinnae worry, son, you'll get there one day."❞

Malcolm Macdonald *remembers the 1974 FA Cup Final*

"Heroes are perfect – Jackie (Milburn) was perfect."

Bobby Charlton

❛Jackie Milburn was a fine player – he was quick, he was fast, he had a change of pace, he could play outside-right or centre-forward.**❜**

Stanley Matthews *paying tribute to a former England colleague*

❝So look out, Hoddle,
we've got Waddle
He takes players on
– it's one big doddle.
And new boy Peter,
runs like a cheetah
Beardsley's gonna
be a world-beater!❞

'Going Up' by Tyneside group **Busker**, *1984*

❝ So Brighton kick off this historic match and, as you sample the quite unique atmosphere here at St James' Park, you wonder how British football let alone Newcastle United will ever replace Kevin Keegan. **❞**

Commentator **Alan Parry***, 1984*

Whatever I've given Tyneside, it's given me a hundred times as much. I hope I'm always their friend and I can tell them one thing – they'll always be my friends up here.

Kevin Keegan's *retirement speech after his final game for Newcastle, 1984*

❝I feel a bit sorry for Newcastle at the moment. Their fans have been fantastic – you can hear them – and their players gave everything today.**❞**

Tony Adams *interviewed at Wembley minutes after he had led Arsenal to the League and FA Cup Double, 1998*

❝It's lovely that he's in charge of his hometown club and that pride just oozes out of him.**❞**

Brian Clough *gets sentimental about Bobby Robson*

❝I'll be bringing the pigeons up to Newcastle with me, but I'll have to bring them up in the car. They're not good enough to find their own way here yet!**❞**

*Bird-fancier **Duncan Ferguson** at his first Newcastle press conference*

❝ I regard this as a system from the Middle Ages. It is really treating men like cattle and really the position is that they are paid slaves. **❞**

Lord Justice Wilberforce *upholds the legal case brought by Newcastle player George Eastham against the maximum wage, June 1963*

❛ We're very happy to have won the Cup. Every man in Newcastle has done his duty. **❜**

Captain **Jimmy Nelson**, *collecting the FA Cup after the 1932 final*

❝I couldn't tell you what the atmosphere is like there now, I don't understand half the players because they are foreign. Now I'm at Villa, I'm the one with the funny accent.❞

A rueful **Steve Watson** *tries to sum up his days under the Gullit regime*

❝ The two seasons we played together at Newcastle were like Heaven. **❞**

'Sir' Les Ferdinand *on his devastating partnership with Alan Shearer*

❝Not a very nice river. Some days you didn't need a bridge to walk across it.❞

*Dunston-born **'Rocky' Hudson** muses on the 'coaly' River Tyne*

❛I'm coming home Newcastle,
If you never win the Cup again
I'll brave the dark at
St James' Park
At the Gallowgate End
in the rain❜

'Home Newcastle' by **Busker**

❝I fancy Liam O'Brien over the wall.❞

Lennie Lawrence *predicts United's free-kick winner in the Wear-Tyne derby, 1992*

❛With all those replica strips in the stands, coming to Newcastle is like playing in front of 40,000 baying zebras. ❜

David Pleat, *then Sheffield Wednesday manager*

❝Is Kenny Dalglish a big girl's blouse?**❞**

Jeremy Paxman *provocatively opens up a Newsnight debate on football managers*

❝ We'll play you anywhere –
Hackney Marshes – we're not
frightened. **❞**

Kenny Dalglish *in a phone call to Stevenage FC
after a rumpus over Broadhall Way's fitness to host
an FA Cup tie*

❝Frank Clark, a left-back, that rarest of breeds, came on a free transfer from Newcastle at the age of thirty-two – the bargain of all bargains.❞

Brian Clough

"We're supposed to be at home!"

Newcastle fans *singing in Barcelona, 11.12.02, after torrential rain saw their game postponed for 24 hours*

The manager said at half time if I got six he might give me a Mars bar. I'll have to go out and buy my own now, won't I?

Alan Shearer *on 'only scoring five' against Sheffield Wednesday in an 8–0 success.*

It was the saddest day of my life: he was my very best buy. I could watch him play all day and every day.

Joe Harvey *on the day knee ligament trouble forced midfielder Tony Green to quit, December 1973*

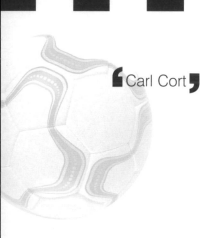

'Carl Cort'

Shola Ameobi, *when asked what Bobby Robson called him*

‟We were a team in the best sense of the word. There were no superstars. No world-beaters, just a damned good team.„

Jimmy Scott, *who played all 12 games in the Fairs Cup-winning run of 1968–69, and scored the club's first-ever goal in European competition*

❛I felt that I understood then what Tyneside was all about – it needed somebody to stick the ball in the net.**❜**

Malcolm Macdonald *reflecting on his home debut hat-trick against Liverpool, 21.8.71*

❝The Newcastle Chairman Sir John Hall went on the record to claim that Les Ferdinand would be leaving Newcastle 'over my dead body' – I wonder if he is still alive.**❞**

Les Ferdinand

❝The crowd sucked it in.❞

Kevin Keegan *claims a communal assist for his debut goal v QPR*

❝In Liverpool you get it from The Kop, but at St James' Park it comes from everywhere. It's like stereo with four speakers!❞

Kevin Keegan *compares crowd noise at two of his favourite clubs*

❝ There's no job in football that I've ever wanted. This is the only job I've ever wanted. **❞**

Kevin Keegan *returns as manager, February 1992*

❝It wasn't like it said in the brochure.**❞**

Kevin Keegan *walks out on United over broken promises, March 1992*

❛Like selling the
family silver…**❜**

Chairman **Gordon McKeag** *on giving up control
of the club*

❝His enthusiasm has and always will be, incredible and always worth a place in your side. Great players like him write their own scripts. **❞**

Kevin Keegan *on the evergreen Peter Beardsley*

❝A great appointment. He obviously loves the club, which is really important. I'm not saying Kenny Dalglish and Ruud Gullit didn't love the club, but Bobby knows the place, because it's in his heart – and I think that is a massive advantage.❞

Kevin Keegan *on Bobby Robson's appointment*

❝We've enjoyed the ride, we've paid the money, got the ride, got off the tramcar – let's go again. We can do better.❞

Bobby Robson *after the Barcelona home defeat ended the Champions League adventure, 2003*

He's got this terrific little engine, I don't know where he gets his petrol from – I could do with some of that.

Bobby Robson *on Kieron Dyer*

❛ They talk about Newcastle being a sleeping giant but it was more comatose than asleep. **❜**

Local journalist **Bob Cass**, *1992*

❝Too busy walking Charlie Mitten's greyhounds…**❞**

George Graham *explains why he never made the grade as an apprentice at Newcastle*

"As soon as I walked into the ground I was greeted by the statue of former striker Malcolm Macdonald."

David Ginola *gets his numéro neufs confused – he of course meant Jackie Milburn*

❝I was worried to death that no one would turn up. Ten years is a long time. People forget. ❞

Jackie Milburn *on his 1967 testimonial. Nearly 46,000 attended*

❝ Craggs forward, Keegan's flick, Varadi, Keegan again – chance here for Keegan… he's done it! Kevin Keegan scores and St James' Park goes absolutely wild! ❞

Roger Tames *describing Keegan's debut goal against QPR in 1982*

> **❝** If I had known in advance of the two years of heartache I faced when I moved to Newcastle, I would not have taken the job. **❞**

Jim Smith

❛He's just handed in a written transfer request. The handwriting was beautiful.❜

Kenny Dalglish *on David Ginola*

❛I queued for five hours at the Gallowgate end to watch Keegan's first match.**❜**

Alan Shearer, *Newcastle fan*

❝ If someone wants to keep something confidential, talking about it in a Spanish brothel is not the way to do it. **❞**

Justice Lindsay *refuses to grant an injunction against the News of the World newspaper on behalf of Freddy Shepherd and Douglas Hall*

❛ Alan Shearer is boring – we call him Mary Poppins. **❜**

A small sample of what Shepherd and Hall wanted to have banned

❛ You know what Newcastle are like. You never know what's going to happen. **❜**

Kenny Dalglish *after a Shearer-inspired 4–3 win over Leicester City*

❝I wanted to score goals at St James' Park. I've lived my dream and I realise how lucky I've been to have done that.**❞**

Injury forces **Alan Shearer** *to retire early, April 2006*

‘Alan Shearer has been the best striker in the Premiership.**’**

Alan Hansen

‌It seemed fanciful to believe that the circle of my life would complete itself with a homecoming at the club I had watched through dazzled eyes as a young boy from Langley Park.

Sir Bobby Robson's *initial reaction to the thought of managing Newcastle, August 1999*

❝ Freddy Shepherd honestly believed that [Michael] Carrick would not move to any Premier League club but Newcastle. **❞**

Sir Bobby Robson, *who wanted to buy Carrick from West Ham United for £3 million in summer 2003*

❝I don't need to be told by anyone that Newcastle are one of best supported clubs around. Everything is geared to be successful, and I hope I can bring success.❞

Graeme Souness *takes over at Newcastle, September 2004*

'Sou long.'

The Sun's *headline when Souness was sacked,*
February 2006

❝I could sign a bad player every day between now and 31 January. There are plenty out there.**❞**

A frustrated **Glenn Roeder**, *January 2007 transfer window*

❛I like to use the word warrior. Warrior means you never give in and he never gives in. He has been in bed for five days with flu and he has lost nine pounds. Most players would have cried off but not only did Nicky play, he started and finished the game and if anyone deserved to score, it was him.❜

Roeder *admires Nicky Butt's match-winning display at Tottenham, January 2007*

❝ People should understand that any player coming to a new country will need to do some settling down. It is a whole new environment: a new style, a new culture and a new way of life. **❞**

Obafemi Martin, *December 2006*

‘ There were three great clubs in the frame but the further it got towards the deadline the more it became clear Newcastle was going to be my destination. ’

Michael Owen *joins the Toon, August 2005*

❝There is no hesitation by the club in recording its sincere appreciation for the way in which Sir Bobby has handled team affairs during that five-year spell which has seen a significant turnaround in the club's fortunes.❞

Newcastle statement, *August 2004*

❛I was about to enter a period of life that I can only really describe as a kind of bereavement.**❜**

Sir Bobby Robson *on being sacked in August 2004*

❝I have had a couple of chats with Kieron and I have been impressed with him. He seems to have matured while he has been battling back [from injury]. In some ways the setback seems to have helped him grow up.**❞**

Steve McClaren *prepares to recall Kieron Dyer for England after a two-year absence*

He's an adopted Geordie and it's great to have him back. He loves the area, the club and the fans, and they love him too. **"**

Newcastle chairman **Freddy Shepherd** *hails the return of Nobby Solano, August 2005*

❝ Nobody seems to know that right-back was my natural position before I moved to England. Kenny Dalglish wanted me to play right midfield when I arrived here. I was very happy to play there and I scored goals, so nobody knew I could play right-back. **❞**

Solano *explains his surprisingly good form as a defender, January 2007*

❝ I'm a very happy man tonight. I know what Jackie means and meant to the people. I can now sleep easy that the pressure has gone. **❞**

Alan Shearer *grabs his 201st United goal in February 2006, breaking Jackie Milburn's Newcastle*

SOURCES: page 5: Paul Joannou 'United – The first hundred years and more', 2000; p6: John Gibson, 'The Newcastle United Story', 1970; p7: *The Newcastle Journal*, June 1957; p8: Internet Bowie fansite, 1999; p9: *When Saturday Comes*, June 1999; p10: Michael Hodges, 'Kevin Keegan – Reluctant Messiah', 1997; p11: ibid; p12: *442*, Feb 2003; p13: *442*, June 2002; p14: *442*, March 2001; p15: BBC TV 'Just Call Me Bobby', Feb 2003; p16: ibid; p17: ibid; p18: 'Kevin Keegan Portrait of a Superstar', 1984; p19: *Sunday Sun*, 2.2.03; p20: *442*, Nov 1995; p21: *442*, Aug 1999; p22: 'Kevin Keegan – Reluctant Messiah'; p23: ibid; p24: ibid; p25: *442*, Sept 2002; p26: *The Mag* fanzine, Issue 8; p27: 1980–81 Newcastle programme; p28: 'Newcastle United – Keegan Newcastle: The Story' Video, 1992; p29: *442*, March 1998; p30: Colin Malam 'The Magnificent Obsession', 1997; p31: 'Kevin Keegan – Reluctant Messiah'; p32: *442*, March 1998; p33: BBC Radio 5 Documentary, 1994; p34: ibid; p35: ibid; p36: 'Kevin Keegan Portrait of a Superstar', 1984; p37: Transworld Sport TV show, 2002; p38: *442*, Dec 1994; p39: *Toon Army News* fanzine, 1994; p40: Phil Shaw, 'The Book of Football Quotations', 2003; p41: ibid; p42: Manchester City website interview, 2002; p43: *442*, March 2003; p44: *442*, Jan 2003; p45: *WSC*, May 2000; p46: *WSC*, Nov 2001; p47: 'Keane – the Autobiography', 2002; p48: *WSC*, February 2002; p49: *WSC*, March 2000; p50: *WSC*, November 1999; p51: *WSC*, Oct 2001; p52: Champions League press conference, UEFA.com, 14.11.02; p53: *WSC*, Jan 2003; p54: *WSC*, Oct 1999; p55: WSC, May 2002; p56: Newcastle press conference, Aug 2003; p57: ibid; p58: *442*, March 2000; p59: *442*, June 2002; p60: Len Shackleton, 'Clown Prince of Soccer', 1955; p61: *442*, Dec 1999; p62: *442*, April 1995; p63: *442*, May 2003; p64: *442*, May 2003; p65: *442*, May 2003; p66: *442*, May 2003; p67: *442*, Oct 2003; p68: *442*, Dec

2002; p69: *442*, March 2003; p70: *442*, May 2003; p71: Matchday programme, Oct 1983; p72: SJP press conference, 30.7.96; p73: *WSC*, Feb 1996; p74: *WSC*, March 1996; p75: *WSC*, Oct 1998; p76: *WSC*, Oct 1997; p77: *WSC*, Nov 1998; p78: Nick Emerson 'Perfect Pitch Volume 1', Sept 1997; p79: ibid; p80: Matchday programme, Aug 1980; p81: 4thegame website, 1997; p82: 4thegame website, 1998; p83: 4thegame website, 1999; p84: 4thegame website, 2001; p85: Press conference, 23.10.02, Ananova.com; p86: *NME*, 2000; p87: FA Commission statement, 2000; p88: Press conference, Ananova.com; p89: 4thegame website, 1999; p90: 4thegame website, 2000; p91: The Kempton Website, 2001; p92: Spursnet unofficial website, 1994; p93: *442*, May 2003; p94: 4thegame website, 1998; p95: *The Independent*, Nov 2002; p96: Century Radio broadcast, Feb 1996; p97: SkySports broadcast, 29.4.96; p98: *The Mag*, Issue 7; p99: 'The Official History of Newcastle United' video, 1991; p100: ibid; p101: ibid; p102: NUFC.com 25.8.99; p103: 4thegame website, 1999; p104: BBC *Match of the Day*, 5.2.72; p105: 'The Book of Football Quotations'; p106: NUFC.com, Nov 2000; p107: BBC Radio 5, 8.11.97; p108: *The Sun*, Sept 1982; p109: *MOTD*, 2.10.82, p110: Paul Joannou, 'United – the first hundred years', 1994; p111: BBC Wembley documentary, 1997; p112: ibid; p113: ibid; p114: 'Going Up' single, 1984; p115: *MOTD* 12.5.84; p116: ibid; p117: Skysports live, 16.5.98; p118: *442*, July 2003; p119: Harry Harris, 'Newcastle out of Toon', 1999; p120: Roger Hutchinson, 'The Toon', 1997; p121: 'The Official History of Newcastle United' video, 1991; p122: 'Newcastle out of Toon'; p123: *442*, July 2003; p124: *Washington Post*, Feb 2002; p125: 'Home Newcastle' by Busker; p126: Live ITV match coverage, 18.10.92; p127: 'The Book of Football Quotations'; p128: *Newsnight*, 1998; p129: NUFC.com, Jan

1998; p130: Brian Clough, 'Cloughie – Walking on Water – My Life', 2002; p131: NUFC.com, Dec 2002; p132: 4thegame website, Sept 1999; p133: 'United – The first hundred years and more'; p134: 4thegame website 2002; p135: 'United – The first hundred years and more'; p136: ibid; p137: Les Ferdinand, 'Sir Les', 1997'; p138: *Shoot!* TV programme, 1982; p139: ibid; p140: 'Newcastle United – Keegan Newcastle: The Story' video 1992; p141: *United* magazine, 1995; p142: *Evening Chronicle*, 1990; p143: 4thegame website, 1996; p144: *Sunday Times*, Sept 1999; p145: UEFA Press conference, 19.3.03; p146: Newcastle press conference, 23.8.00; p147: *Mail on Sunday*, 1992; p148: *442*, February 2003; p149: David Ginola, 'Le Magnifique', 2000; p150: 'United – The first hundred years and more'; p151: 'The Official history of Newcastle United' video; p152: Jim Smith, 'Bald Eagle', 1990; p153: 'The Book of Football Quotations'; p154: *United*, 1996; p155: *NOTW*, 1998; p156: ibid; p157: *WSC*, March 1997; p158: www.bbc.co.uk/football, April 22, 2006; p159: www.bbc.co.uk/football, April 22, 2006; p160: Bobby Robson, 'My Autobiography', 2005; p161: Bobby Robson, 'My Autobiography', 2005; p162: *The Sun*, September 6, 2004; p163: *The Sun*, February 2, 2006; p164: www.bbc.co.uk/football, January 21, 2007; p165: www.bbc.co.uk/football, January 15, 2007; p166: *Daily Mirror*, December 29, 2006; p167: ibid, August 31, 2005; p168: *The Sun*, August 30, 2004; p169: Bobby Robson, 'My Autobiography', 2005; p170: *Daily Mirror*, February 2, 2007; p171: www.bbc.co.uk/football, August 2005; p172: *The Sunday Sun*, January 14, 2007; p173: www.bbc.co.uk/football, February 4, 2006